Love's Labours

Zeeba Ansari is a poetry tutor. She has worked in partnership with Cornwall Adult Education and Library Services, and on a freelance basis. She has edited *The Launde Bag* (2005), *Inspirations* (a pamphlet of poems by Truro Library Poetry Group, 2006) and, with Victoria Field, co-edited *Prompted To Write: Words for Well-Being* (fal, 2007). She has had articles published in *Writing Works: A Resource Handbook for Therapeutic Writing Workshops and Activities,* eds. Gillie Bolton, Victoria Field, Kate Thompson (2006), and *Prompted to Write.*

Love's Labours

Zeeba Ansari

P$_i$ndrop Press

Published 2013 by
Pindrop Press
Mallards
Steers Place
Hadlow
Kent

www.pindroppress.com

ISBN 978-0-9573290-4-1

A catalogue record for this book is available from the British Library.

Typeset by Pindrop Press.

Printed and bound in the UK by Lightning Source.

Cover image: Catherine Hyde, 'Woman and Pear Tree', 2000, acrylic on paper, 24 x 14 inches, http://www.catherinehyde.co.uk

Acknowledgements

Some of these poems (or versions of them) have appeared in
*Ambit, ARTEMISpoetry, Hidden Histories: A South West Poetry
Project*, edited by Greta Stoddart, *Magma, Poetry Wales, Scintilla,
The Forward Poetry Anthology 2010, The Frogmore Papers, The
Rialto*, and *Peony Moon* (www.peonymoon.wordpress.com).
'Blodeuwedd in Cornwall' was highly commended in the Poetry
on the Lake competition 2007; 'Homecoming' was one of the
winning poems in Guernsey's Poems on the Buses competition
2010.

I am indebted to Frances Wood whose book, *The Silk Road:
Two Thousand Years in the Heart of Asia*, has been a source of
illumination and inspiration.

Very special thanks to Caroline Carver and Penelope Shuttle for
their unfailing support, encouragement and guidance.

for Deeba

Contents

I Song's Needle

II Fu Hao Considers the Morning

I

Song's Needle

Love's Labours

She said *bring me something useful and wonderful*
so he caught the wind and tamed it to his hand.

She held down her fluttering robes, saying loudly
over the din, *this is not enough*

so he sank below fathoms of light and found the place
the sun went when it slept, and brought it to her

and she said (catching his ankle to stop him rising)
this is not enough, so he went deep in an owl's wing

to the blades in an owl's heart
that settle on the painful world as snow.

He brought them to her, shivering on the tiles,
and she said *this is not enough*, so he crafted a country

from ivory and she peered close,
saw cranes flying south, and said *this is not enough*

so he stood before Death and said *what more can I do
to show my love?* Death said *I am both useful*

and wonderful, so he returned with his guest
and she nodded, said *yes*, but by then it was too late.

Mistley Pond

Send her into the cold house
to steal the silence standing in a tub of weeds.
Or drink the deep water
and lie down, a goblet brimming with lilies.

Divert the river from her body to the grass.
Let it flow out in the devil's name.
Or irrigate her breast like fatal good fortune.

Let her tread the sky with a broken neck
and folded wing. *Or breathe her last*
earth-bound with sorrows.

Let her go uncrossed to a box
in a room of rain. *Or let her children mourn her.*
The box will be broken by hooves and wheels,
the gravestone grow finer with age. *Both*
will turn their faces from the people and disappear.

Mistley Pond in Essex was used to test those accused of witchcraft. If they
sank, they were believed to be innocent; if they floated, they were guilty.

18

Persephone

Four months in the dulse of dark
she comes up moist and firm,
fresh as a puck of goats' cheese.
She dries her skin, takes her place
at the head of spring, breaks
the sky's bread, makes grace
of sun and rain before a supper
seasons long. When mist and fog
begin to salt away the days
her mother cries, and sends her back
in nettle leaves and tears of whey.

dulse: a type of seaweed used in preserving foodstuffs

19

Fire Song

When the stromkarl sings
a witch lights her heel with the oil of dusk
and shines nightlong the steps of the dance
but morning has a village voice
whose twelfth is a strain of fire
so keen it cuts the lacing of her ribs
and marvels at her naked heart
as the wind runs her lips
from the hall of her mouth
whose tongue is a child lost
in the burning cantref of her face.

Engraver

after an illustration in Foxe's Book of Martyrs
of the burning of Bishops Ridley and Latimer, 1555

He cuts them out of shadow,
out of flame. No matter
how they love and hope
he fills their lips
with ink's thin smoke,
drawing them upwards
with a stroke, each hand
a cruse containing prayer,
each holy sleeve a gust
of sparks the roller blows
across the plate. Fire scores
the hard flat surface
of their hearts, and each man
says *he makes the mark*
to free our souls
which flow to heaven
in a wax of words –
be of good cheer,
and play the man
says Latimer, who knows
the engraver's grasp
on life, like other men's,
is never truly sure
and finds, in chasing
human wickedness,
a gainful way
of steadying his hand.

You May Be Secretary of State, Walsingham,

but what obsesses you is bringing the mind
to the bliss of breaking, the steady scrub

of pain in the house of bone
till even the words of fools come up gold.

Your fingers are kings of the body's court
whose slightest look dismisses the heart

to the heart of its worst imaginings,
your eyes masters of the long freeze

burning into adulterers, forestallers,
dice-coggers and liars letters that hang them.

England for you is ice, a brilliant black,
but Mary was the longest winter

and *God restore the true fire of me*
you sang as her heretic head lapsed

from its neck. Elizabeth's was the flat-iron
of Latin, but that dead red mouth spoke French

and you never forgot how its movement
serviced your itch.

Bliss, Walsingham, jammed upright
in your night-time's white-hot gown

screwing out your own confession. Bliss.

'God restore the true fire of me' – Jack Clemo

Duty

She's at the table washing spuds
in answer to the rain, scraping piles of carrots.

Her kitchen is full of dying flowers and steam.
Stacks of washing in a basket.

Her stockings are blue and faithful
to the cold. The window breathes out

mist and spiders, her sweat. She's a good girl,
but when autumn pats the bed

off she goes. They love each other so hard
trees come down and fall across the sheets

but her conscience treks from field to house,
crosses signs and pavements, to fill her lap.

Traffic has been hazardous, it says,
and I am thin with toiling. She thinks

of her mother taking the days carefully,
the months resting in their leaves.

Her work isn't finished. She holds gravel
in one hand, rosemary in the other. From gravel

she pulls a brown fish. From rosemary, a pen
of lambs. She tidies her hair and pushes the window wide.

The basket in the corner fills with onions.

Shaman's Daughter

Her song's needle sews goodness in the air
bringing meats of strawberry,
nuts and corn, clear water of honey.
She stirs the rain to a silver brew
the land drinks deeply,
wipes the ground with fire
so summer's hide will grow.
She knots a kith of clover leaves
to put down blood roots,
strings a crop of sky on willow
to give the weather a lovely eye.
Her father's face is dark.
She waits for his return.

Love's Disciple

The hills are steep and my load is heavy
but wherever I go I give thanks to you.

I kneel in a roomy pen among white goats,
sprinkle a quickset hedge with balsam water.

I stand in a small thatched hut and sing to my lyre
while a weeping woman wreaths a shrine

to the Mare-Headed Mother in freshly gathered roses.
In rich men's houses I rub myself with oil

and pray at tables heaped with every kind of food.
I give coin, plate, gold-embroidered robes,

valuable necklaces. I offer barrels of wine,
milk, barley and wheat flour. In leaner months

I gather small change and sometimes silver.
In every district the people welcome me

as your disciple. Your temple is only
as strong as the heart it supports

and round it I am constructing a tall fort
of wattles fastened on a timber frame.

Mare-Headed Mother: the Gallo-Roman fertility goddess Epona.
Parts of this poem were found in Robert Graves's translation of
Apuleius's The Golden Ass.

25

Lleu

He lies with a woman whose voice draws blood
from the wind, locks him fast
in a white field where a sharp moon kneels,

gauging the shot of light it needs for killing.
Hit between the sinew and the bone
he takes a spear's span of love through shirt

and chest – his fame rests between the barrels
of a bathtub and a buck goat
who lead his world away from land and water –

dying, he cries *my sickness was made*
by a woman whose heart
searched far and deep for the englyn of graves.

englyn: a Welsh verse form

Blodeuwedd in Cornwall

The world is a stone with a hole in it showing two people walking in
the woods at Malpas, one with a carrier bag, the other a peaked cap and
a cloak fastened with a green stone. They're skimming spears over Truro
River, warming up on ships with names like *Kylie* and *Boy-Willy*. She has
a belt of flowers, he's drinking from a bottle of beer and sand. They're
dragging a bathtub with a goat in it hung from a full set of horns. There's
something pan-footed about the pair of them – she's beautiful, but goes
in and out with the sun, he's standing on a mountain watching the rain
come down singing. When they pass, the smell's unique – wet manors
tainted by horse dung and noise, blood feuds, Benylin, chewing gum.

The world walks through the woods and turns the pair like goldfish
in a plastic bag. I lift my hand, thinking to make a cut and burst into their
story. But they'll choke on air so I nod without a word, not even a boozy
couplet from a brown bottle. Let them sit under a tree on their carrier bag
and eat sandwiches and suckling pig. The river carries sprigs of broom,
meadowsweet, flowers of the oak swift as the scent of spears through
a man with one foot on a goat's back, the other on water.

Fantasia on a theme of birds

Wrens fly from the breast of the dark
into an ageless day,
                    curlews float songs for the light
downriver –

the drone of water underfoot
                    is time at its deepest pitch.

*

Here among lines of wind and gorse
                    a stonechat sets its heartbeat to the sea –

above, a lark in an endless sky
                    sings beyond season and sight.

*

Turn from the coast to a country lane,
                    noon sun warming phrase after phrase
into swallows,
                    blue-black rondo of an evening rising
to notes composed entirely of air:

swifts, in a coda of dusk.

*

At the end of each movement   night,
pacing through twilight
                    to an owl's dark measure –
the soul's *da capo*,
                    its return to the beginning
before that long rest deep in the wing.

Yggdrasil

She soothes the world
with a rattle of flesh and bone,
holding it to her heart
until it stains the front of her dress
with sleep. The timer tells her
Mimir's head is done
so she lifts out the comb of his tongue
and curries the sweetness
into a harp. She sings out the night
till the stone in her pocket
turns to light, then goes upstairs
to the tree she rode
nine days and nights
to make her good eye
worse, her bad one better.
The boughs in her bed
are black with ravens
with beaks like mussels
dripping fringes of oats
and barley, salt gardens
whose wisdom is way to the north,
high-walled and growing up weeds.

Atonement

When she drowned he warmed the heart
of a willow and put it in her chest.
She weeps as she sets beer and meat for his supper.
When night darkens her grain, he shivers.

When she was buried he cooled the hottest flame
and set a diamond in her. She turns in the sun,
filling his sight with perfect women. At night
she puts on such a light he can't get near her.

When she was burned he mingled her ashes with salt.
He dug for the oldest stone, polished it with language.
She grinds her body against him, cries as the moon rises
like yeast for the simple bread of loving.

Conejo

The tilemaker of Majorca is sometimes given
to firing greater things – a century,
the birth of love, flowers from the lips

of gods. Big-armed, warm-faced, he works
in woman's clay, and comes into the café
his hands rosy with breasts. *Women*

provide my strongest red, he says
as he fishes a star from his beer
and gives it to me. *Taste,* he says. I taste –

warm light runs through the star-shaped tile.
Conejo, he says, *we make them here*
and here you are, in white and blue,

a Spanish rabbit on my kitchen wall
with sorrows of your own. His fingers
stirred the last house in the square

too deeply, brought out love and loss –
leaving, he wept himself white as cheese,
his tears a gloss for the deep *azûl*

he took from the sky he walked back in.
His firing went to the tile's heart
who roars out *egg-layer, mound-thumper*

calling out the dead when March is luting
lightly as a gun and longs to break its strings,
be *Mister Hare* and net the ghosts

in his round blue eye
but I tell him *not yet, it's February,*
drinking time for the soulless dark

quaffing the month with a dirty mouth
and looking, cold smith, to fit
a new frost to my English spring.

31

Chatelaine

The linen chest opens soundlessly
on the said and done, men's lives

now washed and pressed
in deep preserving salts, rinsed of the silk

and rot of loving. This one's skin
was lousy with excuses – she scrubbed

to make it soft and whole, a shirt
his wife would never recognise.

That one's children wept so much
his heart saw floods and ran from them,

making a tear no stitch could mend –
her patient hands patched up the threads.

Another lived alone for fifty years
and blamed so hard blood stuck to it –

her fingers soaked away the cloth
till the stiff soul finally dropped.

And this one came naked and prepared
with folded clothes, a cold ring finger,

the world sewn up.

Saviour

He saw men silenced by war, raised them from their blood.
Each night he covers them with stars, says *this will do.*
They kneel, say *because you have done this,* and their hands adore him.
She sees, casts dung on the fire to foul her sight.

He saw the blind country walk into the sea, led it back with his hand.
A root in the gullies of men, he flowers in unexpected places.
In women's work, looms blurt out the riches of silk.
She throws her spinning wheel into the well.

He nurses the harp back to its strings, the viper to its glancing
        take on things.
The world cries to be mended by him. She knows this, keeps notes.
Each full page she tears out and eats. With such a ready belly
she'll give birth soon, but who will love her child?

Mrs Bates
To Her Husband Travelling in Santarem, Brazil

The confluence of the Amazon and Tapajos
is a pleasant place to live if you are not sat
at your writing desk in starched and glorious
whites, the cool hand of the chair at your cleft –
there are no insect pests, mosquito, sand-fly
or motuca and at this moment a beetle
a house fly and a flea are fighting over
the heart   the blood   the chitlings
of my very tender English north-lit skin.
Are they so sweet there, soft in the pore,
or does the cat-tongue sun start licking them
even as they drip from the womb? *The climate*
is glorious; during six months of the year
very little rain falls and this is the hat and heel
of your dilemma – you carry the dry spell
in a bottle round your neck, together with
the sweat of all the women and the flight
their breasts attain *and the sky is cloudless*
for weeks together particularly when you
on your back are following every star's skirt –
here, the moon is a fountain in a courtyard,
my cupped hands drink its lunar light –
fresh breezes from the sea moderate
the heat of the sun which, taken in quantity,
sings me a noon-song you'd hardly recognise,
my skin the purest of notes on the air,
silk keys my hands play for days together –
the wind is strong for days together,
it is difficult to make way against it –
I do not try, it enters the windows and doors
of the house with a key made
from one of my ribbons, *scattering*
loose clothing in all directions
especially downwards. After a breeze
I am well loved and there is, my friends
remark, a glow to my face. After a storm
I am not fit company. *The streets are clean*

and dry, even at the height of the wet season
which, most distant of loves, I go through now
and now and now – your clean dry streets
are not enough to stop the flood. *Fresh fish*
can be bought in the port on most evenings,
and very good bread is hawked and my fingers
make the finest bakers, queen of yeasts
they are so in touch we rise together
and take a turn around the town,
where we shop for milk to coat the cry
in the back of my throat. *Finally, there is*
delicious bathing wet weather collects
in my heart the leaves blow in – *when the east wind*
blows a swell rolls in on the clean sandy beach,
and the length of the swell is longer than
our separation. I hear there is no fear of alligators.

The words in italics are taken from an article in The Guardian *of
1.9.07 by Tim Radford, who quotes from the Victorian explorer
Henry Walter Bates.*

35

Finn

In the pan the holy fish whines
songs of melting fat, browning skin.
At every strophe its head turns
further into smoke – air splits its tongue –
the damn thing spits hot oil
and foresight, blistering his thumb.
He sucks quicksmart on fishy *jus*
whose tartness plants a perfect kick
on his mind's backside, punts him
from his tree and drops him
in the outraged arms of Finegas,
who sizes up the mighty leap
the boy took, follows, falls,
lies ruined in the dried-up stream.

Leda

She stands in her coat at the bus stop
hearing him wish her good health
and good wheat. He says
the wind has countless tiny bones
which sweep over a country in rain
and set it singing.
                    On his bed
he blows her hair softly and poems
come down. She blinks in the light
of his back as he opens his wings,
loses herself in slow storms of birds
rising from lakes.
                    It's late.
Her purse holds a field of wheat,
her head a swan's eye. No bones
in her father's voice as her mother
dries her coat. The reek of marsh
stands over them and sings
of what she's done.

Homecoming

So down he jumps,
shaking his salt-legs,
his bartered rugs of kelp
and the epiglottis
of the oldest sailor in the sea
wrapped and singing on his shoulder,
his pipe a small smoked fish,
his heart a tobacco plug
mashed by the long walk
up the cobbled hill
to the door flying open and her voice
like oil gone mad in the pan
at the grin pouring
from the wreck of his head.

World Tree

When he left, she hung like Odin
nine days and nights
in her bed.

Ravens shat on the headboard.
The room became white.
Roads in her ribs
grew black and wind-fed.

She nursed feldspar and quartz,
dead eggs of granite.

She turned in her sleep
and stone struck stone. Sun
flew in a phrase of light,

burning old mouthfuls
of mist from her pillow.

Her eyes opened.
She woke with his words
gone from her side.

These, she says, are the things I learned.

Love was a man of blood and honey.

I drank from a cup not stirred
or seen.

His shirt was a harp of plenty.

I took my tongue from the pocket
and restrung it.

His tie was a hawk rising
from the oldest tree.

I stripped blue clothes from my back
and wore the loose linen of roads.

His shoes were wells of the world.

I worked the soft leather of rain
and shod the earth.

Marriage Interview

Your mouth has lies in it as big as barns.
Grist for our mill, he grins, *and if you're wise*
you'll come to my lap right now

and have the grumble taken out of you.
Sugar and apples make a good pie,
but too little salt means a pudding lacks spice

and leads to a life looking better behind
than it does in front. *I'll make perfect pastry*
to last from goodnight to good morning.

What can you do with the planks of the heart?
Knock them into a nursing chair,
rock back and forth and fill its arms with babies.

Can you make cheese? *I can make milk in the teat*
come warm and blue. Can you catch a horse?
I can whistle a mare at a town's distance

and she'll meet me with washed feet.
What do you pray for? *You, and you*
telling me your fruits are three times

ripe for eating. What about the calendar
of heaven? *I'll cover your holy days*
with kisses. And the common rules of love?

Better ask forgiveness than permission.

Marriage

Sit down with me
where the common rivers meet,
smooth your clothes, become a bird in the rushes.

Soak the thorn
of your throat in spikenard,
consume your sharps and let us fold up

the corners of our quarrel.
We were fledged to plainness of word
and look, our love has become a part of speech

we can't agree on,
shepherds herding with the same crook
branch or bough, stream or brook, white herald or storm,

tipping scorn
on each other like salt
from the truck of the sea. I see a flat-topped

hill whose sides
run down so rampantly the heart
has little grip. You see a set of skills, widow

of medieval rules, a perfume jar, a gauntlet.

Water

You are no longer with me. You exist only
in rainy weather, in sedges, at the fringes
of clouds. Remember the river bank?
You stood, looking down, and said
here in water's native land
words flow to the wadi of meetings –
your lifted finger stirred a crowd of gnats
to a second's world at sunset.
We held a ceremony for our dreams;
the last light presided; what we said
was heard by every living thing.

Your words were made of the air –
they passed through sunlight and could not last,
they were ghosts and passed over water
so could never rest. How was I to know
each word would be overlooked by silence?

*

This river has a guilty mind –
it remembers the time we lay at its side
and you showed me what comes
of picking the flowers. When I ask it to flow
now as it did then, it sits on its hands
and refuses to move. When you told me
somewhere in our lives we'd meet for good,
I believed you. How can I believe
the world as it is?

Forgive me this silence
you said, and wove your voice into the leaves –
I have closed the eyes of heaven to promise and fame
and sit like a swallow in the rain,
waiting for the spring to hear you again.

Legacy

Four thousand years ago she finds her bones in a jar of burnt peas.
She brings them out, rubs together the sticks of her tongue and a clear sea
comes. The ocean is a pure note from which the light is pouring.

Two thousand years ago she finds her body in a field of beans. The beans
travel through her navel, small hearts in the hollow of her hips growing
upward to the air. Where her belly meets the soil the crops begin.

A thousand years ago she finds her voice. Her body stands by, marvelling.
She exults, and bridges spring up in her throat and from them words
great as air, a wing for whole cities.

Today she starts living. She collects rain, seawater, tears, kneads them
with a heel of salt and myrtle. Over them she puts a dishcloth, covering
the edges of the world. The planet is her clean kitchen and in it she's rising.

Sheela-na-gig

A ceiling boss has little use for legs
but she has two and a hole between so deep
they tried a bucket but it never came up,

so deep they pleaded with the sea *go in*
but it never came back. Between the drop
of roof and floor she thumbs a ride from silence,

twitches on a root of alum and a rude man's spittle,
couched and marvellous in lessons boys
learn under her with mirrors in their faces.

She had a lover once, who brought a silver flute
and played the tunes her father played,
whose mouth was the O her mother made

when she came out. Her young man blew too heartily –
she jigged, he slipped. Candles were lit,
she never found the flute, but visitors catch

a gleam when they look up. The locals know
her place is over water, under stone, but strong beer
makes them wonder what she keeps in there –

she'd write a note in brandy if they gave her a cup,
apply the lines like gauze and let them soak up
all the fingers poked, the widened eyes, the smiles –

if they gave her a cup her tongue would grow
bigger than bronze, and speech would fall out
full as eggs and wide enough for wedding bells.

Sleep

The last dream-visit, he lashes his tail so hard the water-glass
breaks. She's soaking wet *and this* he says, *is the pool I drink from.*
Her nightdress catches in his claw and he holds up the torn dark cotton
and this, he says, *is the forest I walk in.* She fumbles for the switch
and the light snaps on *and this*, he says, *is the mouth I eat with.*

Fifteen

At the far end of my heart is an island.
The people who live in this country are called
my first years – they have their own stories

of how the world was formed and how they came to be.
These, they say (their voices come faint from afar),
are tales of wonder – like most things of this kind

they can't be explained. Old women now,
their eyes are opaque as they sit round the fire
which for clarity's sake is where I am now

at forty-three. How did they come to be?
They were *just so* (though my mother and father
find it hard to keep quiet in the shadows) –

don't ask, they say, why at one year old
we crawled to a place we couldn't get out of,
at four we noticed the wind, at nine

the need for more space in the soul for sorrow
way back in the time of the heart
that was endless and flat and waiting for me

to run in at fifteen and start pushing it up
till I fell on my knees underneath just staring.

Tent

As a child in summer you founded a country
whose native sun was the dim green light

of your tent in the garden, its local squares
laced up each night, its villages listening for rain.

When you slept, orchards rose from the apples
you kept in your pockets, peaches grew

from a heap of spat-out stones, oceans
gathered in the ground-sheet. As morning

collected in the flaps, you went to the woods
to search for twigs to whittle into tent pegs,

hand-picked keepers of your borders. Now
when you sleep, the same woods wave

their passports at me – at the checkpoint
you're guard, driver, smuggled human goods –

our bed has become a foreign land
and nothing I say is understood.

You keep me at a distance, in the dark,
far from your capital city. To make the word

husband you hired a man who broke stone,
mixed cement, and raised it facing north.

What you meant was four corners lightly set on grass,
a windproof canvas under stars.

Mari Lwyd

Don't turn your back on her, old time,
wooden dad shouldering her skull
for sight of wind and weather –
let your tongue's sharp twig
frighten the life into her
at midnight, sole minute of the world
her heart remembers –
shake her bonce as you'd shake salt so
seconds fall from her dead white mane
into open houses and, poor singer,
let her croak at the o'clock
like a bad ballad,
no leg to stand on but rhyme.

Walking Man

His hat's a courtesy to the miles
roughed by boots whose feuding
is like brothers testing themselves
on flinders and tarmac, beetles,
nails, chewing gum, dogshit.
The world's his boxing ring,
he bruises its eye
and carries a bloodied cheek,
alliterates the low long living he keeps
as he seats himself, saying *I here endeth*,
dousing his knees in shade
before heat splits the pegs of his arms,
and always in glints like a hare
is the horizon which stands round every bend
and the forecasting stars
he doesn't try to believe in, just walks
the heel off his head
for his heart to silken like hill-water,
his song strive like salmon
at the rising, terrible instinct of home.

Below Stairs
Cornwall

Under glittering skirts she's bare
and shaking down plums of quartz

opening a cabinet of caves
for the doctoring sea to examine

holding out handsome arms
for long tattoos of serpentine.

The tide breaks down, tells her it loves her
as the years do, courting her face

out of its doorway of thrift, running
deep rings round her, asking again

for love, not duty, but she dries herself
and dresses neatly for the long walk

up from the earth, shaking seawater
from her mantle as she leads out

young men and women schooled
to serve – tin, the bright one,

soft-faced slate, maker of rooftops,
mason of the grave. Granite

has taken the lesson to heart and stands,
wild stone, still as moonlight, child

of two fathers and broken by each . . .
overhead, underfoot the tide is passing.

The Sea Courts the Land

She stands on the beach as he salts his breath
with songs from which a red gull flies – sunrise,

bruising his skin as she turns away
to the white wedding face of the cliffs.

See what I offer, he calls, *a bedspread so fine
you'll never feel it,* but as he approaches

she holds up her hand. Through it run strata,
land-inspired winds, a thousand dry churches.

He's surrounded by fools. The moon's no use,
her milk throat closed, her temper chancy,

the clerical tide gone under to write up currents.
He posts himself to her in a tanker

but she holes him on rocks which split his liver
which oozes oil – she tells him *break*

and he collapses against her hard white palm.
She speaks calmly as she unscrews his last rivet,

so soft a voice his bolt's already shot
by what she whispers –

*land, boy, land is your cradle and coat –
you're under the heel of great ships,*

*the horizon's your master, the sky a bagman
selling you shore to shore.*

Thalassa on Guernsey

All day you work, salt poet singing the journeys of men
from island to island. Your house is built on four corners
of foam, with window panes of bright and cloudy weather,
a roof of wind. Oceans move under your scullery, lapwings gather
in the light behind your eyes. The names of your children
are Lissroy and Jethou; Brecqhou and Burhou play games
in the sand with the turn of the tide. The food at your table
is the grain of the sea; you look out on a wood of water.

Men wax and wane; you watch them row to the brittle stars,
note their passing with a pen whose heart is water,
its nib mist. Your words are stepping stones
to bays where the heart can haul up in bad weather.
When storms break the bindings of the shore
you turn the last page and read what's written there.

Men Scryfa

If there was a dossier   of how the world looked
when ships were tuned   to the key of stars
and men sang, spat,   turned in their sleep
as the watch saw things   he could never put in words,
it's long gone. Look in   painted caves, among ammonites,
drag the sands for   drowned churches – time after time
the eye recedes   till all that's left
is a stone in a field   telling me here was a young man
who is part of a dream   and the wind binds him
and round him cattle make marks   that are erased by rain.

II

Fu Hao Considers the Morning

Kashgar Market

In the crowd a girl wearing red brocade boots
chats to a merchant
who praises her eyebrows – so young in her boots,

too young to see those who've passed through
on their tough little horses,
riding away with the sun.

Her father's eyes are failing; among carpet-traders,
sellers of spices and salt,
he seeks horizons small enough to fit his hand.

He's ridden for years to return to the light
of an earlier spring, where a girl with bare feet
is patting the neck of a tough little horse,

lifting her head to catch his eye –
if she chooses to live for ever
let it be with him.

The wind has a pearl in its mouth,
the wind has a voice he's ridden for years to find:
when life's long vowel finally breaks

he'll return to the light of an earlier spring
when love walked out of the desert
and stood barefoot by the well, waiting.

Silk Road

He's on a journey made by hand, his breath and blood
hum to the click of the shuttle –
                                    a road is being spun
and on it a man in black robes, riding a donkey.

Snow is falling, a delicate weft spreading over his path –
his head runs lengthwise, his heart across,
                                    twin threads
drawing old age and winter into his cloth.
                                    He dreams
of apple blossom under a straw-coloured sun,
wonders what will happen when the weaving is done.

Weaver at the Caves of the Thousand Buddhas

Entering the temple caves
he finds the past cocooned in seamless rolls –
his moist breath parts the air in a thousand strands,
from one long thread he weaves a heaven,
spins out across mountain and water the cloud brocade of night.

On a delicate loom cities grow: pale Bokhara, star of silk,
Hamadan, whose ribbon-like passes he knots by hand.
No god in splendour wove a finer garment for the light –
from Tyre to Chang'an in slow procession its people come,
the last an old man breathing gently on the sun in his hand.

Crescent Spring

Time holds no *pentimento* of the past –
all is water,

silver nerve running through
the ghost of a man in the act of becoming

the million ways light falls on him –

he calls out from the mouth of night
sisters, lovers, brothers, fathers,

folding the rich hours round them again
as if they have no shadow.

*

The past is a man returned to water –

his son peers out from behind a camel's legs,
sees an angel descend to the pool to drink.

The boy shifts – she lifts her head –
heavens reform in her eye.

*

The man wipes his mouth to stop time passing.

His name for the moon means *bad faith*,
god of death who wouldn't leave the world,

his name for the sun is *wife*.

*

Night dissolves in the water's eye
its quarters of dusk, its dark bazaars –

the man looks up and sees
souls rising to the level of the light,

milky centuries slide by
dropping their cloudy rains.

Echoing-Sand Mountain

At the foot of Mingsha Shan
the quarters of time come together
in silence,
waiting for winds to recover
warm shadows who know
where the lost words of travel
are buried.

Each grain of sand's
an empty house whose rooms
a dry wind wanders through,
carrying souls from the stone of heaven
to meet their ghosts.

Spirit armies draw their swords
and from the mountain's side
cut a poem fresh enough to drink;
dead moons touch the heart of cities
caught between cry and prayer.

At the foot of Mingsha Shan
hope has changed hands many times –
let the wind recover its voice, just once,
before dying.

Fu Hao Considers the Morning

Three thousand years from here
Fu Hao considers the morning.

Her cricket-strung fields are singing:
sun is her head-note, moon is her spirit;

the two form a cross she will never set down.

*

Light is a peacemaker, returning to perfection
the million drops of sand shaken

from the muzzles of mountains
bending their heads to the White Jade River

where silk roads find reflection.

*

Darkness is fluent in words of the earth
silencing songs of armies

sending their fire through the clay of the world;

the singing stops, becomes time pressed
in the shape of a carving

cold in the hand of a queen.

*

Fu Hao considers the flowers of the world –
their heads of jade, their heart-stones

close as night lays love-stones on her skin:
sun rises; light is her monument, the last thing.

A Wood Engraving of an Official and his Servant

He finally has time to count the stars, though never arrives at
the same number twice; has faith in his black velvet slippers;
is troubled by the draught round his ankles, which is tied
in the knot of time the engraver made as the door opened
and his wife offered tea.
                                    He wonders what she makes of him
as a work of art, will never know what she wrote in her letter
which remains in the hand of the servant standing behind him,
thankful never to meet his eye.

Lord of the Six Ways

The Lord of the Six Ways is preparing to leave the world
and asks his painter to draw him seated in the house of silence

but the painter's heart is lodged in the house of fire
and here among wet poplar leaves and the mud of the courtyard

he sees only brightness. The Lord says *paint sorrow*
but his brush is made of faith, its ink and colour pure radiance.

The Lord is displeased; the world he has studied two thousand years
is made not only of light, he says, but that which runs through

and holds things together. The painter's hand trembles
on a fragment of joy lodged in the throat of the brush;

all the death in the world won't clear it. He paints a glass bowl
which the Lord picks up and turns; travellers crossing the desert

look up to see the sun. The painter says *Lord, look at their lives;*
hairpins and flowers hold things together

as do markets of indigo, jade, black salt, yellow plums.
The Lord of the Six Ways says nothing. His body is lodged

in the house of earth; it is two thousand years since he saw it.

At Quanzhou Harbour

Sunset fires the ghost fleets of the Dragon Throne,
their hulls smoke like parchment;

dusk chars timbers, its lingering stain
a wind in their sails, which blacken and curl;

the ships become paper, floating downriver
as boats a man made for his son, who cries in delight;

become burnt letters sending word to his wife,
who looks up from reading –

he stitched sea and sky to the spine of the world,
making a scroll whose pages fly open

as if in a whirlwind – horizons unfold in her hand.

The years turn east; he writes with the limitless ink
of the sea how his heart misses the simple things –

a shoot of green rice, the delicate claw of the first crane
touching the fields in spring, his boy singing –

on his wife's lap a grey cat is reading the sutras –
the scroll springs back; the ghost ships sail.

Home

I have seen the Caliph's tree of gold and silver,
held night-and-day tablets engraved
with the world. I have watched the moon
drown her light in Crescent Spring,
draw from the water's throat that which
water would leave unspoken. I have been
to the place of no return to see the girl
who lost the key to a house of treasure
made by a god for a weeping soul –
and what have I learned? That love
is the body's light; the heart beats faster
to see walls and a roof of lattice and mud,
a woman running down the road
with a child in her arms.

Lady of the Silkworm

A woman diving for jade
finds love –

she hides it in her hair,
keeps it secret for hundreds of years –

when she dies, it goes with her into the tomb.

For centuries wind blows on it,
storms rage around it, sun bakes it:

the seam of the heart begins to show.

It's found by a king; like one asleep
he stumbles blindly,

falls on his knees and lifts it from the sand.

He wraps it in felt and carries it home –
heated in crucibles

no gold shows; questioned by thinkers
it stays silent; put to death

it remains unscathed. The king
shows his wife, who takes it in her hand

and patiently begins unwinding the strands.

Night Climbs the Tian Shan Mountains, Pursued by Day

The world puts out a clear black root
and she climbs,

each step a faint note rising higher –

halfway up she hears the cry she made
when she ran off yesterday,

shoeless and shirtless, into other countries,
taking them to bed –

at the head of the dark   the moon flies to her fingers,
smelling the musk of stars.

Day follows, sure-footed, his pale cloak grown
round flight-hollow bones –

his blunt fingers stain the mountains
saffron and rose,

ink and colour   brushed over the earth –

as he reads from a roll of yellow paper
his sutra, the sun,

she steps out of her belt of stars
and vanishes before the morning light

which long ago plotted a path inside her.

Archaeology

A world is searching for its people –
it pauses, stoops,
                digs in the sand like a dog,

brings up a bronze food vessel,
runs light round the rim
                like a moist finger –

lost voices cry of fears and desires
until the day fades;
                words run down
the dark, to silence.

Guinea Worm

The barber works to remove a worm
a river long – the market shrinks
to a steamy room,
he uses his fist to rub a circle, clear his eye –
and what an eye he has! –
that surly ewe becomes
a fat-tailed sheep of Samarkand,
its fleece a glowing jade –
coins in his pocket
are poplar leaves at Crescent Spring –
beyond the city grasses grow
in lengths of divers kinds of silk,
the plains a stiff brocade –
sunset warms the sky
with red hides brought from Russia –
stars are spices falling softly, collecting in
a box on a belt at his waist:
he wakes to the knowledge
summer is coming –
he must make his final journey
as the sun is rising.

Burial Ground, Astana

Their lives no more than folded paper
small enough to fit a pocket –

north and south roads meet
in the lines of their hands – here's snow

two fingers thick, a clear spring shaped
to the curve of the miles they've ridden –

when found, they offer
new models for the miracle: warm books

made from folds of the desert
a moon's width across

clouds of local paper   rolled up for storage

history's watermark   on their faces
coldly written stories of the mountain.

Last Thoughts of the Poet Wu Ming

My writing room is the early morning,
my mind a book of waking and breathing,
                    its pages stained with light.

At night I lie awake, kept from sleep
                    by the open eyes of poetry.

*

My fingers shake,
                    scratching the delicate world;
the dried bed of the Khotan river
                    swells and flows,
brims with waterbirds
sweet-water pools, vast reed-fields.

*

The desert lies at the end of every sentence.
A light wind stirs the delicate brushes of firs;
what they write on the sky
                    is only for the sky to read.

*

One bird celebrates the dawn much as another,
                    music to make the lost men sing.

I take comfort from this.

I have passed the inn of the long day
                    in the company of night.

I should be glad of the pain of light.

'the open eye of the poet' – Tony Harrison

Ascent to the Stone of Heaven

At the top she hesitates –
her singing-robes will fill with moths,

she'll become an absent figure,
the blind side of a temple banner –

somewhere near the end, she thinks,
the earth will speak, his wife will answer,

earth and heaven move together,
saying as she chafes his hands

the loss of a country is easy to bear.

*

China stands, an empty house –
she turns back briefly: mists lift;

time's atmosphere is clear enough
to see through the eye of the ordinary world

to an ageless day
when deserts remembered

how water comes back from the dead.

*

The loss of a country is easy to bear –
simply a matter of letting it fall,

walking the foothills in her skin,
drinking snow water as she climbs

beyond the kingdom of daily life.

She won't weep for the world
as she steps from its keep, into the hold of the sky.

Notes

Part One

Fire Song: a stromkarl is a Norwegian spirit who has eleven different music strains, ten of which people can dance to. The eleventh is his night strain, which makes everyone and everything dance. A cantref is an ancient administrative division of the Welsh counties.

Lleu, Blodeuwedd in Cornwall: In Welsh myth, the magician Gwydyon conjured a woman of flowers, Blodeuwedd, as a wife for his ward, Lleu. Lleu could only be killed when he stood by the river Cynfal with one foot on a bathtub and the other on the back of a goat, and then only with a special spear. When Blodeuwedd fell in love with Goronwy, he killed Lleu in this way. For this crime, Blodeuwedd was transformed into an owl.

Yggdrasil, World Tree: in Norse myth, the tree in whose branches Odin hung for nine days and nights in order to learn the secrets of the dead. Mimir was a man renowned for his wisdom; after his death, Odin preserved his head and consulted it for advice.

Finn: in Irish myth, the poet and sage Finegas waits patiently to catch the Salmon of Knowledge. When he finally does, his apprentice, Finn, cooks it. Fat from the pan burns his thumb; he licks it, absorbing the gifts Finegas sought.

Sheela-na-gig: a carved figure of a woman displaying a greatly enlarged vulva. Found on churches, castles, and other buildings.

Mari Lwyd: in parts of Wales, the Mari Lwyd (*Grey Mare*) is borne through the streets on New Year's Eve by a party which stands in front of every house singing traditional songs. It consists of a mare's skull (sometimes wooden) fixed to the end of a pole; white sheets fastened to the base of the skull conceal the pole-bearer.

Men Scryfa: 'written-stone'. This standing stone in West Cornwall marks the burial place of a warrior who died in battle.

76

Part Two

Kashgar Market: Kashgar is a former crossroads of Asia, where the north and south Silk Roads meet.

Crescent Spring: a crescent-shaped oasis in the desert in Gansu province, China. *Pentimento:* the reappearance of an earlier painting due to a wearing-away of the layers covering it.

Echoing-Sand Mountain: Crescent Spring is set within the Mingsha Shan, or Echoing-Sand Mountain, an area composed of high dunes. Mingsha Shan is named for the sound of the wind whipping off the dunes. Legend has it that during a battle a great gust of wind buried the soldiers in sand, where they continue their fighting. Another story relates how, returning from battle, soldiers passing Mingsha Shan complained of thirst; their general thrust his sword into the mountain and water sprang forth, forming Crescent Spring.

Fu Hao Considers the Morning: Fu Hao (d. circa 1200BC) was one of the wives of King Wu Ding of the Shang dynasty; unusually for the time, she was also a (highly successful) military general. Her tomb contained over 750 jade artefacts.

At Quanzhou Harbour: in her book *The Silk Road: Two Thousand Years in the Heart of Asia*, Frances Wood notes that in Chinese the term for a cat purring is 'the cat is reading the sutras'.

Lady of the Silkworm: Empress Lei-tzu (or Si Ling-chi, 'Lady of the Silkworm') is credited with discovering silk-making. In around 2640BC, she developed the process of reeling - silkworm cocoons are steamed or placed in warm water to soften the natural gum, then unwound. Each cocoon can give between 2,000-3,000 feet of filament.

Guinea Worm: Ella Christie describes in some detail the removal of guinea worms by barbers in Bokhara market place in the early 1920s, the larvae having been ingested with stagnant water and grown up in the body cavities of unfortunate sufferers. The adult worm usually emerges from the skin of the lower limbs and has to be removed in stages, wound round a stick.

Burial Ground, Astana: The Astana Graves are a series of underground tombs in Xinjiang, China. The tombs were used by the inhabitants of Gaochang from 200AD-800AD. Due to the arid environment many artefacts have been well preserved, including natural mummies.

Lightning Source UK Ltd.
Milton Keynes UK
UKOW04f0811090913

216800UK00001B/13/P